Open-ended Questioning:
A Handbook for Educators

Robin Lee Harris Freedman

Addison-Wesley Publishing Company
Menlo Park, California • Reading, Massachusetts
New York • Don Mills, Ontario • Wokingham, England
Amsterdam • Bonn • Sydney • Singapore
Tokyo • Madrid • San Juan • Paris • Seoul
Milan • Mexico City • Taipei

Also in the Assessment Bookshelf:

Authentic Assessment: A Handbook for Educators
by Diane Hart

Managing Editor: Michael Kane

Project Editor: Mali Apple

Production Manager: Janet Yearian

Production Coordinator: Claire Flaherty

Design: John F. Kelly

This book is published by Innovative Learning™, an imprint of the
Addison-Wesley Alternative Publishing Group.

ISBN 0-201-81958-9

5 6 7 8 9 10 - ML - 97

This Book is Printed
on Recycled Paper

Contents

Acknowledgments

Thank you to the CAP for permission to adapt and use copyrighted materials from *Golden State Examination, GSE Chemistry, A Question of Thinking: A First Look at Students' Performance on Open-Ended Questions in Math,* and *Writing Assessment Handbook, Grade Eight.*

Books are not written in vacuums or back rooms. They evolve with the assistance of many people. I would like to thank:

My colleagues at Fort Bragg Middle School for sharing ideas;

My science colleagues for believing in and encouraging me;

My students for writing responses to open-ended questions week after week, year after year;

Bob Tierney for asking, "So what are you doing now?" after my first book was published;

My editor and encourager, Mali Apple—she kept me active;

And my husband, Lee, for editing, proofing, and being the wind beneath my wings.

Open-ended Questions:
A Student-centered Approach

Authentic assessment methods assess, among other things, students' abilities to use higher-order thinking skills to express content knowledge. Open-ended questioning is a form of authentic assessment, and allows students to use higher-order thinking skills through a variety of writing styles.

Open-ended questions usually consist of two parts: a prompt and the directions for writing. The prompt sets up the writing situation as a pre-writing activity, and it may be a cartoon, map, graph, quote, or diagram. The directions for writing keep the writer focused on the topic and writing style.

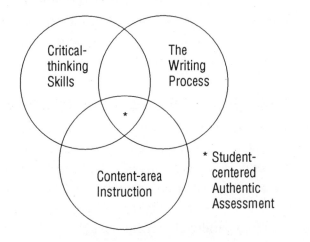

Student-centered authentic assessment occurs when critical-thinking skills, the writing process, and content-area instruction are combined and used in open-ended questions.

Teachers, like other humans, are judgmental creatures. We go through life evaluating events against the criteria of our preferences, standards, or experiences.

***Linda Nott,
Colleen Reeve,
and Raymond Reeve,***
Middle-level Educators[1]

For example, a traditional essay in an art appreciation class might ask the student to compare the painting styles of realists and surrealists. An open-ended question on the topic might look like the following:

The prompt: Imagine you can travel through time and space, collecting artists and their works. You travel back in time to pick up Leonardo Da Vinci and Pablo Picasso, then travel to the Louvre in Paris to examine their paintings. (Of course your time machine instantaneously translates everything they say into English.)

The directions for writing: Write the conversation these two artists have as they compare their paintings. Have them converse about six paintings (three from each artist) that you select from your class work. Remember, you have a realist talking with a surrealist. How are their painting styles different? How are they similar? Use your best conversation-style writing.

Using open-ended questions for assessment allows students to express their own ideas. The example above assesses more than content knowledge: it assesses students' abilities to synthesize information. Responses to open-ended questions will provide you with insight to your students' conceptions, misconceptions, strengths, and weaknesses.

Open-ended Questioning and Thinking Processes

While improving students' thinking abilities has been a learning objective for one hundred and sixty years, only since 1980 have United States educators made this objective a specific goal.[2] Educators who teach higher-order thinking skills need to assess such skills accurately. Students can acquire and practice many thinking skills in a variety of content areas.[3]

By their nature, open-ended questions assess writing, conceptual understanding, and thinking skills—especially students' abilities to analyze, to evaluate, and to solve problems. The model presented in this book is based on this idea.

Open-ended Questioning and the Writing Process

When answering open-ended questions, students write as a means to an end. They express their thoughts through at least four different writing styles. These styles—mechanical, transactional, expressive, and creative[5]—engage students in different thinking processes so that they are challenged to think diversely. Since writing becomes an extension of students' thinking, you can assess their thoughts through their prose.

The chart below gives examples of the writing styles students use and, according to Bloom's Taxonomy, the level of understanding needed to write in that style.

Writing Styles and Understanding		
WRITING STYLE	EXAMPLES	TAXONOMY OF UNDERSTANDING
• mechanical	• dictation, copying	• knowledge
• transactional	• note-taking, summaries, comparisons	• comprehension
• expressive	• journals, letters, narratives	• application
• creative	• stories, plays, fiction	• analysis

Open-ended Questioning and Content-area Instruction

Open-ended questions often reveal more information about student understanding than "traditional" testing methods. You can use open-ended questions to check for conceptual under-

Critical reading, writing, and thinking must be taught across all disciplines . . . these processes are essential, but often difficult for both teachers and students if they have never thought of writing as a powerful device for learning itself.

Jan Talbot,
History–Social Science Consultant[6]

standing before, during, and after instruction. They are a tool for pre-tests, homework, quick checks for understanding, exam reviews, end-of-unit exams, and even long-term research.

What Students Think of Open-ended Questions

Students respond to open-ended questions honestly and with insight. When asked to comment on open-ended question assessments, students were candid. They didn't always like answering the questions, but you will see in the following responses from middle and high school students that they appreciate the flexibility of open-ended questions:

> *"I personally liked your kind of test much better because people in general can use more creativity to write philosophically (write your feeling about the subject instead of just the facts) instead of black-and-white answers that the teacher wants to hear."*

> *"I thought that they were easier—because you could write about what you want. It's not like math where there is one right answer. You follow the main subject, but you can have your own ending and beginning. I'm not worried about anything—because I know I can do a good job. You have to know the science; you don't have to know all the facts."*

> *"I dislike it because I'm not a critical thinker and these are critical questions."* (This student scored a B with her "non-critical-thinking" responses.)

> *"I like the essay because it made me think about what I really know. I also like the fact that the questions to the essay were easily explored and some helpful clues were given to kind of guide us to the conclusion."*

"I like the essay because it was adventurous. It helped my mind to visualize and expand and understand. It made test-taking less stressful, because you share your own opinion."

"I liked this part of the exam because it's a change from the normal. It causes you to reflect back on what you have already learned and apply it in a different situation."

"I found myself liking the essay questions. They seem to be a way to think about the problem presented in class. And they're also a good learning tool."

Writing Open-ended Questions: A Quick Glance

2

Follow these five steps to success when writing open-ended questions:

1. Look over your curriculum.

See what concepts or topics lend themselves to open-ended questioning formats (such as those presented in Chapter 3). Make a list of two or three ideas. Select places to use open-ended questions during your unit, such as a pre-test, a post test, research, a check for understanding, or an activity follow-up.

For example, suppose your class is working on a waste management unit.[1] Three key concepts are:

- Recycling preserves natural resources.
- One-directional nutrient flow causes several problems in waste management.
- The use of nonrenewable fossil fuels creates pollution.

2. Based on the critical-thinking skills you wish to assess, choose one questioning format.

Ask yourself: Will your students interpret data? Will they write conclusions based on previous work? Will they describe? Will they solve a problem? (See Chapter 3 for details on the questioning formats.)

For example, in your unit on waste management, you decide to assess your students' abilities to solve problems. You choose the problem-solving writing format for assessment of the concept "one-directional nutrient flow causes several problems in waste management."

3. Write the first part of the writing prompt—a description of the situation.

Title it. Include information that will motivate students to write. (See Chapters 3 and 6 for sample open-ended prompts.) For the example, you could use the writing prompt:

Re-use: One Dump's Revival

You have joined a local planning committee for the re-use and reclamation of materials previously discarded in your local dump. Assume that there are no hazardous or radioactive wastes in your dump.

4. Write the directions for writing.

Be specific about what students should write about. Define the writing style and include specific content and concepts that you want described or explained. (See Chapters 3 and 6 for examples of directions for writing.) For the waste management example, you might write:

Directions for writing: Write a plan to recover usable materials from your local dump. Instead of allowing one-directional nutrient flow, follow the ecological principle of recycling nutrients. State several positive effects and give reasons for them. As you develop your plan, keep in mind pollution reduction, resource depletion, nutrient use, and energy requirements.

5. Develop a simple rubric.

Rubric development is a focusing process. A rubric lists expected responses in the areas of conceptual understanding, content knowledge, critical-thinking processes, and communication skills. (See Chapters 4 and 6 for more on rubrics.)

Your waste management example rubric could look like this:

Re-use: One Dump's Revival			
GENERAL AREA OF ASSESSMENT			
CONCEPTUAL UNDERSTANDING	CONTENT KNOWLEDGE	CRITICAL-THINKING PROCESSES	COMMUNICATION SKILLS
SPECIFIC CHECKS FOR UNDERSTANDING			
• one-directional nutrient flow causes several problems in waste management	• nutrient cycles • energy flow • replenishment of nutrients • depletion of resources	• speculating about effects • problem solving	• conciseness • organization • precise and varied vocabulary • effective grammar and usage

After following the above steps, present your question to your students. Grade it. Save a range of responses to use as benchmarks—examples of different levels of achievement—the next time you use your question. See Chapter 7 for a closer look at the process.

Questioning Formats

3

In one traditional approach to essay questions, teachers present students with a two-part question called a *writing prompt*. The prompt is used to capture student interest and to describe the nature of the writing assignment. The first part gives pre-writing information, and the second part gives directions on the writing style. Sometimes the writing directions are incorporated into the prompt section. Open-ended questions easily fit this essay-question format. The diagram on the next page visually illustrates the overlap of thinking skills, Bloom's taxonomy, and the open-ended questioning formats.

Formats for Open-ended Questions

The six questioning formats described in this chapter are developed from several commonly used English writing prompts and call for higher-order thinking processes. These questioning formats—analysis, comparison, description, evaluation, fiction, and problem solving—will each be explained below, with a description of the thinking strategies used and examples.

Questioning format: analysis

Analysis defines something by describing what it is, what it isn't, what it ought to be, and what it implies. Students form opinions and make judgments every day. Their maturity level depends on

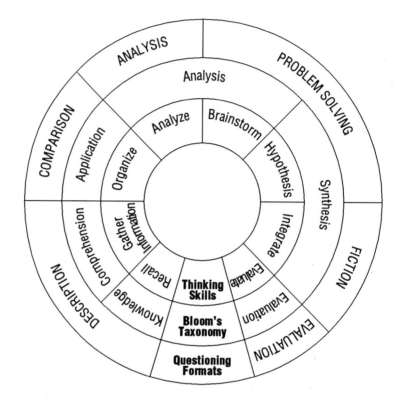

This chart shows the connection of thinking skills and Bloom's Taxonomy to the six open-ended questioning formats.

their ability to see multiple perspectives, to consider casual evidence, to arrive at a logical conclusion, and to make plausible predictions. Analysis essays challenge students to visualize the whole of an idea, to pull it apart, to examine its parts, and to explain it bit by bit.

Thinking strategies used in analysis writing

- Perceiving several points of view
- Weighing evidence
- Making logical conclusions
- Showing plausible relationships
- Identifying attributes and components, relationships and patterns, and main ideas

Samples of analysis writing

- Commentaries, book reviews, and directions
- Sequences of events
- Data analyses
- Explanations of how something works

Example using an analysis questioning format

After a combined social studies and science unit on acid rain, students are asked to analyze the situation presented in the question below.

Acid Rain Task Force

You have been asked to join a task force on acid rain. Your job is to analyze the situation in your area and to prepare a complete report to the committee. After your laboratory work on the effects of acids on freshwater habitats, and your own extensive research, you sit down to write.

Directions for writing: Your report should include data collected from around the county, results from your personal lab work, and a summary of current research. Remember that you are not trying to persuade the committee to act; you are giving them a detailed analysis of the current situation of the effects of acid rain in your area.

Questioning format: comparison

A comparison shows how things are similar and how they are different. It illustrates how things change over time, shows how processes differ from one another, or demonstrates how something unfamiliar resembles something familiar.

Because writers must know the facts about items to compare them, comparison essays are useful in assessing student knowledge. More mature writers can compare multiple characteristics.

Thinking strategies used in comparison writing

- Grouping and comparing by multiple factors

- Given lists of characteristics, dividing items into groups and generating new lists of characteristics
- Organizing factual information

Samples of comparison writing

- Writing that groups, orders, serializes, and sequences events, processes, and ideas
- Guess-who or guess-what descriptions
- Before-and-after case studies
- Debates, prophecies, and predictions
- Responses and rebuttals
- Product comparisons

Example using a comparison questioning format

After completing a study of energy, students are given the writing assignment below.

Energy Travels

In our unit on energy, we have learned that energy, in the form of heat, travels by conduction, convection, and radiation.

Directions for writing: Compare these three methods of travel. Be sure to include information about molecular motion, states of matter, and temperature. Give examples of each kind of travel.

Questioning format: description

Description explains things using the five senses. The writer may write in two distinct styles. In *observational writing,* the writer, as an observer, describes an event or organism from objective observations. This style draws heavily on the use of the five senses. *Report of information writing* appears in most magazine and journal articles. The writer organizes data, research, and observations into a report. This style conveys information instead of expressing or changing an opinion. You will see this style often in this book.

Thinking strategies used in descriptive writing

- Compiling and explaining experimental techniques and writing step-by-step descriptions of processes
- Writing conclusions, speculations, and descriptions based on extensive observations
- Gathering and organizing observations

Samples of description writing

- Journal entries and who- or what-am-I's
- Letters, speeches, interviews, and newspaper and magazine articles
- Product comparisons
- How-to's, directions, and procedures
- Essays and poems

Example using a descriptive questioning format

Students have just finished a unit on mineral identification. This descriptive question challenges their ability to organize and to describe their new knowledge.

WANTED: Mineralogist for Mars Colony

While reading the latest want ads for the Mars colony, you spot an ad for mineral detectives requesting someone newly trained in the identification of minerals. You decide to call the 800 number. The recruiter tells you to submit a short essay titled "How to Identify Minerals."

Directions for writing: Keep in mind your latest laboratory work with minerals. Remember, your scientific equipment will be limited because of the cost of transporting it all to Mars. Include only what you will need to make an accurate identification of the minerals found on Mars. Assume that Mars has several of the same minerals we have on earth.

Answer the following questions in your descriptive essay: What tests would you perform to identify the minerals you find? What scientific equipment would you take with you? How will you check the accuracy of your identification methods?

Questioning format: evaluation

Evaluation focuses on the supporting evidence: facts, figures, data, expert opinions, and research. The writer uses evidence and reasoning to make a judgment.

Thinking strategies used in evaluation writing

- Making value judgments based on facts and figures, not on opinions and conjectures
- Organizing information and making firm judgments
- Clarifying issues and terms

Samples of evaluation writing

- What ifs
- Taking a stand's
- Evaluations
- Decisions on an issue

Examples using an evaluation questioning format

Students in a general biology course answer this question as a culminating project.

The Cell: Up Close and Personal

Imagine that you have the ability to freely travel around inside plant and animal cells. Spend some time examining both plant and animal cells from the inside out.

Directions for writing: After your journey inside both plant and animal cells, choose which one you would rather be. State your decision and support it with reasons and evidence. Include at least three reasons that are supported by research information in your response.

In a social studies class, the group has just finished a unit on industrialization and the formation of unions. Students draw conclusions and support a stand about unions by the answering the question below.

Unions in 1870

You're a worker in a factory in 1870. Knowing the risks involved with unions, would you be willing to join one?

Directions for writing: Write an evaluation essay. State your judgment on whether you would join a union. Support your judgment with evidence. Consider your current working conditions. How might those conditions change with the presence of a union? How might your employer react to your joining of a union? What economic factors might influence your judgment?

Questioning format: fiction

Fiction writing demonstrates the ability to synthesize information in an imaginary context. To write effective fiction, students must be observers and recorders of information. They must also be researchers, for a good story has depth and shows a writer's understanding of a subject or concept.

Thinking strategies used in fiction writing

- Synthesizing information
- Observing, recording, and communicating information in story form

Samples of fiction writing

- Plays
- Science fiction
- Stories

Example of a fiction questioning format

Eighth-grade students answer the following question as an on-going project during an integrated science unit.

It's an Explorer's Life

Pretend you are returning from an interstellar journey. It is your responsibility to write a description of the biome(s) you found on a planet you visited.

Directions for writing: Include information about the living and nonliving components of the biome. Be sure to note food webs, food chains, altitude, rainfall, soil types, latitude, and any other important information. You may wish to attach drawings of flora and fauna, as all excellent xenobiologists do!

Questioning format: problem solving

Problem solving is a specific kind of analysis. The writer describes and analyzes a specific problem, proposes a solution, and tries to convince the reader that the solution is feasible. Depending on the content area, the writer uses several different strategies to show knowledge of the ability to solve problems; for example, algorithms, simulations, speculations, or experiments.

Speculation about causes and effects is a type of problem solving used in essay writing. Given a specific event, the writer predicts possible causes or outcomes of a given situation or experiment. Speculation can range from a wild guess to a prediction based on data and previous experience.

Thinking strategies used in problem-solving writing

- Recognizing a problem using a variety of sources
- Synthesizing information
- Clarifying terms and issues
- Making generalizations

Samples of problem-solving writing

- Cause-and-effect analyses
- Hypotheses
- Letters on local issues, editorials, and speeches
- What ifs
- Proposals
- Interpretations of data

Example of a problem-solving questioning format

This assignment was used in an issues-oriented science/social studies core course to assess students' prior knowledge on how community action plans work.

Pollution: Right Next Door

You recently discovered that the nursery and garden shop next door to the school has been storing several barrels of banned pesticides on their property. You have been named chair of the community action committee to investigate this problem.

Directions for writing: Describe your action plan. Let these questions guide you during your research: What will you do? How will you determine the extent of the pollution? What kinds of experts will you call on to assist you with designing your action plan?

Exercise: Write Your Own Open-ended Question

Repeat this writing exercise for each of the six questioning formats.

1. Choose a topic or concept from a unit you are teaching now or plan to teach soon.

2. Read through the descriptions of the six questioning formats. Decide which critical-thinking processes you want your students to demonstrate.

> Writing is a proven way to enhance student ability to apply and integrate history–social science knowledge.
>
> ***Peter Kneedler,***
> *Research and Evaluation Consultant*[1]

3. Choose one of the six questioning formats.

4. Write a situation in the questioning format you chose. Keep the prompt focused on what you are doing in class, and try to relate it to your students' frames of reference. This is the first part of the writing prompt.

5. Write the directions for writing. Define the questioning format. Include specific content and concepts that you would like described or explained.

Grading Open-ended Questions with Rubrics

4

Rubrics are established procedures and sets of criteria for scoring student performance. When several states began experimenting with authentic assessment, they discovered that new forms of assessment needed new forms of grading. The National Writing Project has been credited with the first use of the term *rubric* for grading schemes. Derived from the Middle English word for red ochre, rubric refers to the color—often red—of the first letter on a manuscript or book page, which was considered the most important. How-to directions were also often printed in red to make them easier to locate. It is appropriate that modern-day grading scheme nomenclature refer back to a red-lettered, established rule.

Elements of a Rubric

Open-ended questions generate a myriad of student responses and require their own grading schemes. Rubrics are sets of predetermined standards that cover several levels of student achievement and are organized to assess multiple learning factors concurrently.

A rubric spells out the criteria for different levels of achievement based on a set of standards that you design. The standards may include *benchmarks,* performance samples that serve as comparisons for calibration. Using these standards, you can separate student responses into different levels of achievement, from a dichotomy to six or seven levels. Here is a five-level achievement scale rubric.[1]

Five-Level Rubric		
	ACHIEVEMENT LEVEL	PAPER HAS ALL OR MOST OF THESE CHARACTERISTICS
4	Exemplary	• is concise, well organized, consistent, complete • is clear (reader does not have to guess writer's intent) • has precise and varied vocabulary
3	Standard	• is well organized • has generally clear intent • has sufficient detail
2	Apprentice	• is inconsistent but adequately organized • lacks detail • presents the basic idea • does not have clear intent (reader must guess writer's intent) • uses imprecise vocabulary
1	Novice	• is not adequately developed • is generic; refers to assignment hastily in a roundabout way • has little or no detail
0	No Achievement	• is blank or unreadable • does not address the topic

With the rubric, you assess various components of the student's knowledge. The components described in this book include conceptual understanding, content knowledge (which changes for each curriculum area), critical-thinking processes, and communication skills. The components appearing in a rubric depend on the format of open-ended question asked. By adding more columns, you can assess additional aspects of students' knowledge.

Creating Your Own Rubrics

You can design a rubric simply by organizing your topic or concept objectives onto an achievement chart. The generic rubric below has several guiding questions you can use to set up your first rubric.

General Rubric Showing Multiple Factors			
GENERAL AREA OF ASSESSMENT			
CONCEPTUAL UNDERSTANDING	CONTENT KNOWLEDGE	CRITICAL-THINKING PROCESSES	COMMUNICATION SKILLS
STARTER QUESTIONS FOR EACH RUBRIC LEVEL			
What are the big ideas?	What are the facts, illustrations, descriptions, and examples the student should have internalized while studying the big idea?	What kinds of thinking processes is the student engaged in while answering this question?	How well can the student communicate? Has the student paid attention to grammar, style, and usage?

Once you have organized your objectives, decide how many levels of achievement you will acknowledge. Also decide whether you will demand complete mastery and whether you will grade students more than once, allowing them to change their level of achievement.

I found my students had an exact idea what constituted a good paragraph. When we graded their first efforts, they were appalled that they didn't come up to their own standards. Now they scarcely glance at the rubric for a good paragraph; they write them.

Seventh-grade English Teacher

Using Rubrics to Grade Student Work

There are two ways to grade student work using rubrics: analytically and holistically. In an analytical approach, the student receives a separate score for each section of the rubric. The completed paper receives a total score made up of individual scores. With analytic grading, students receive their individual scores and get an in-depth knowledge of their achievement.[2]

For example, in a four-part rubric that grades conceptual understanding, content, critical-thinking processes, and communication, the grades could be: excellent (E), can improve (C), or needs some help (H). The matrix of the rubric would look like this:

	Sample Rubric Matrix			
	GENERAL AREA OF ASSESSMENT			
GRADE	CONCEPTUAL UNDERSTANDING	CONTENT KNOWLEDGE	CRITICAL-THINKING PROCESSES	COMMUNICATION SKILLS
E	• excellent conceptual understanding	• excellent content criteria	• excellent organization criteria	• excellent communication criteria
C	• can improve conceptual understanding	• can improve content criteria	• can improve organization criteria	• can improve communication criteria
H	• needs help with conceptual understanding	• needs help on content criteria	• needs help on organization criteria	• needs help on communication criteria

The student might receive a grade like this:

Conceptual understanding	E
Content	E
Critical-thinking processes	H
Communication	C

A holistic approach evaluates the total work as a blend of its individual parts. Students receive one grade for their response. The grade reflects how they performed in conceptual understanding, content, critical-thinking processes, and communication skills combined.

It may take you more time to score a set of open-ended questions than other assessments. To score the papers fairly, you should try to read them all at one sitting. Keep your rubric handy, and keep in mind the general areas of response; in this case, after reading student's responses, you may wish to adjust the rubric.

Using your rubric as a guide, separate student responses into two preliminary categories of performance. Then go back through the papers and divide them into the number of levels of achievement you designated in the rubric. Save several samples of student work for use as benchmarks for further reference.

Once you have finished ranking papers, it's time to award points. For each division or level of response to the rubric, assign a number of points. Award the most points to papers that show the greatest comprehension and expression in all assessed areas. If a student does not respond to the question, award minimal points for effort. Humor might also be rewarded. If a student can make you laugh and show understanding, why not honor that talent?

After you have awarded points, ponder these questions:
- What did you learn about your students' understanding?
- What might you re-teach?
- How will you change your open-ended question for next time?
- How will you modify your rubric?
- Did you give your students an adequate introduction to the process of open-ended questions?

An earth science teacher with twenty years in the career found surprising results with his first use of open-ended questioning. "The essay questions allowed the students to delve into the subject matter in a way that reflected their conceptual understanding," he said as he summarized the experience. "They clearly showed the material I had presented in class and the emphasis I had placed on the topics. They have allowed me to view my section on crystals as being incomplete and as having very little closure. I'll have to expand this section with more lab-oriented activities. The time element in grading had me worried, and it did take more time to grade, but it provided me with a base knowledge of their understanding of the material presented in class."[3]

Detailed Rubrics for the Questioning Formats

What follows are detailed sample rubrics for each of the questioning formats presented in Chapter 3: analysis, comparison, description, evaluation, fiction, and problem solving. Use them to get ideas for your own rubrics. (Conceptual understanding is not detailed in all of the sample rubrics because it is very content-specific.) The thinking strategies related to each questioning format are included as focusing points for each format.

Analysis

Thinking strategies assessed in analysis writing

- Perceiving several points of view, weighing evidence, making logical conclusions, and showing plausible relationships
- Identifying attributes and components, relationships and patterns, and main ideas

A General Analysis Rubric		
	GENERAL AREA OF ASSESSMENT	
CONTENT KNOWLEDGE	CRITICAL-THINKING PROCESSES	COMMUNICATION SKILLS
	CHECKS FOR UNDERSTANDING	
Reasons and evidence	Perceive several points of view, weigh evidence, make logical conclusions, and show plausible relationships	Text, diagrams, and charts
6 — The writing: • gives several reasons and evidence • develops several examples for each area of analysis	The writing: • defines the four areas of analysis: what it is, what it isn't, what it ought to be, what it implies • uses one or more strategies to show understanding: definition, description, examples, illustrations	The writing: • is coherent • is directional • is purposeful • is complete, with a beginning and an end • is integrated
5 — • gives several reasons and evidence • develops at least three areas of analysis	• defines all four areas of analysis • uses one or more strategy to show understanding	• is coherent • is developed • is complete, with a beginning and an end
4 — • gives several reasons and evidence • develops at least two or three areas of analysis	• defines three areas of analysis • lists all four areas but does not define them	• is organized • is complete, but end may be hurried

A General Analysis Rubric (cont.)

	CONTENT KNOWLEDGE	CRITICAL-THINKING PROCESSES	COMMUNICATION SKILLS
		CHECKS FOR UNDERSTANDING	
	Reasons and evidence	Perceive several points of view, weigh evidence, make logical conclusions, and show plausible relationships	Text, diagrams, and charts
3	*The writing:* • gives several reasons and evidence • develops at least one or two areas of analysis	*The writing:* • shows simple understanding of analysis • may not separate all areas into distinct relationships	*The writing:* • is weakly organized • is simple and may follow prompt order
2	• gives several reasons and evidence • develops at least one area of analysis • may list without development	• describes the problem • may not separate areas of analysis distinctly	• is weakly organized • is brief
1	• may list reasons and evidence	• follows prompt • shows limited description of problem	• is poorly organized • is brief
0	• shows no attempt	• shows no attempt	• shows no attempt

Comparison

Thinking strategies assessed in comparison writing

- Grouping and comparing by multiple factors
- Given characteristic lists, dividing items into groups and generating new lists of characteristics
- Organizing factual information

A General Comparison Rubric			
GENERAL AREA OF ASSESSMENT			
CONCEPTUAL UNDERSTANDING	CONTENT KNOWLEDGE	CRITICAL-THINKING PROCESSES	COMMUNICATION SKILLS
CHECKS FOR UNDERSTANDING			
Controlling idea	Information	Similarities and differences	Texts, charts, and diagrams
6 — *The writing:* • clearly states controlling idea • is consistent	*The writing:* • identifies objects carefully and accurately • uses several strategies: facts, details, examples, anecdotes, explanations, definitions	*The writing:* • compares two or more items • details the items • uses several strategies to show comparisons: side by side, lesser to greater, simple to complex, one to one, sequencing, or ordered by a particular property	*The writing:* • is well organized • begins with helpful orientations • is coherent and clear • focuses on well-developed components
5 — • clearly states controlling idea • is consistent	• gives relevant information • uses several strategies	• compares two or more items • details the items • uses several strategies to show comparisons	• is well organized • has an effective beginning and end
4 — • clearly states controlling idea • is consistent	• gives general information • is arranged and grouped logically	• compares two or more items • details the items • uses some strategies to show comparisons	• is organized • effectively begins, yet ends hurriedly

A General Comparison Rubric (cont.)

	CONCEPTUAL UNDERSTANDING	CONTENT KNOWLEDGE	CRITICAL-THINKING PROCESSES	COMMUNICATION SKILLS
	CHECKS FOR UNDERSTANDING			
	Controlling idea	Information	Similarities and differences	Texts, charts, and diagrams
3	*The writing:* • simply states the subject	*The writing:* • gives less information than a score of 4 • lists characteristics but may not elaborate • may give opinions	*The writing:* • compares two or more items • details items • uses a few strategies to show comparisons	*The writing:* • is weakly organized • follows prompt order
2	• simply states the subject	• shows little development • gives few specifics • is brief	• compares two or more items • uses at least one strategy to show comparison	• is weakly organized
1	• simply states the subject	• shows little development • gives few specifics • is brief and very general	• compares two or more items • uses at least one strategy to show comparison	• is poorly organized • is sometimes incoherent
0	• shows no attempt	• shows no attempt	• shows no attempt	• shows no attempt

Description

Thinking strategies assessed in description writing

- Compiling and explaining experimental techniques
- Writing step-by-step descriptions of processes
- Writing conclusions, speculations, and descriptions based on extensive observations
- Gathering and organizing observations

A General Description Rubric			
GENERAL AREA OF ASSESSMENT			
CONCEPTUAL UNDERSTANDING	CONTENT KNOWLEDGE	CRITICAL-THINKING PROCESSES	COMMUNICATION SKILLS
CHECKS FOR UNDERSTANDING			
Controlling idea	Information	Information strategies	Texts, diagrams, charts, and drawings
6 *The writing:* • states a controlling idea • is consistent, focused, and coherent	*The writing:* • includes specific information: facts, details, examples, anecdotes, explanations, definitions	*The writing:* • includes several strategies: personal anecdote, create a scenario, differentiate, group, classify, explain	*The writing:* • is well organized and focused • is well developed, with specific information • is complete, with a a beginning and end
5 • states a controlling idea • is consistent	• includes specific information, but not as much as a 6 score	• includes several strategies	• is well organized • is not as clear as a 6 score
4 • states a controlling idea • is consistent	• includes information, but is generalized	• includes several strategies	• is not well integrated • effectively begins, but may end weakly
3 • simply states the subject • may state opinion instead of giving information	• generalizes • may list things but not elaborate	• includes some strategies	• is weakly organized • may follow prompt order

A General Description Rubric (cont.)

	CONCEPTUAL UNDERSTANDING	CONTENT KNOWLEDGE	CRITICAL-THINKING PROCESSES	COMMUNICATION SKILLS
	CHECKS FOR UNDERSTANDING			
	Controlling idea	Information	Information strategies	Texts, diagrams, charts, and drawings
2	*The writing:* • simply states the subject • may state opinion instead of giving information	*The writing:* • generalizes • gives few details	*The writing:* • includes few strategies	*The writing:* • is brief • shows poor organization
1	• simply states the subject • may state opinion instead of giving information	• may be opinions with no information	• includes one strategy	• is brief • shows poor organization
0	• shows no attempt	• shows no attempt	• shows no attempt	• shows no attempt

Evaluation

Thinking strategies assessed in evaluation writing

- Making value judgments based on facts and figures, not on opinions and conjectures
- Organizing information and making firm judgments
- Clarifying issues and terms

A General Evaluation Rubric		
	GENERAL AREA OF ASSESSMENT	
CONTENT KNOWLEDGE	CRITICAL-THINKING PROCESSES	COMMUNICATION SKILLS
	CHECKS FOR UNDERSTANDING	
Reasons and evidence	Makes a judgment	Voice and style
6 *The writing:* • gives reasons for evaluation, and the reasons clearly justify the judgment • focuses on reasons • gives one or more reasons supported by evidence	*The writing:* • describes the subject being evaluated • states a firm, clear judgment	*The writing:* • is coherent • is directional, with purpose and closure • is fresh and original • is detailed • is well presented • is convincing
5 • gives reasons for evaluation • focuses on reasons • gives one or more reasons and supports them with evidence • is not as detailed as a 6 score	• describes the subject being evaluated • states a firm, clear judgment	• is coherent • is well written • is somewhat predictable
4 • includes a reason or reasons to support judgment • develops at least one reason moderately, but not as detailed as a 5 or 6 score	• identifies the subject • expresses a firm judgment	• is well written • is somewhat predictable

A General Evaluation Rubric (cont.)

	CONTENT KNOWLEDGE	CRITICAL-THINKING PROCESSES	COMMUNICATION SKILLS
	CHECKS FOR UNDERSTANDING		
	Reasons and evidence	Makes a judgment	Voice and style
3	*The writing:* • lists reasons but does not develop them • shows understanding	*The writing:* • expresses a judgment	*The writing:* • is predictable
2	• may list one reason • may describe the subject being evaluated	• expresses a judgment	• is perfunctory
1	• may list one reason	• states a judgment, but only describes the subject briefly	• is flat
0	• shows no attempt	• shows no attempt	• shows no attempt

Fiction

Thinking strategies assessed in fiction writing

- Synthesizing information
- Observing, recording, and communicating information in story form

A General Fiction Rubric		
	GENERAL AREA OF ASSESSMENT	
CONTENT KNOWLEDGE	CRITICAL-THINKING PROCESSES	COMMUNICATION SKILLS
	CHECKS FOR UNDERSTANDING	
Theme or main topic	Development of situation and characters through synthesis of ideas	Narrative aspects and strategies
6 *The writing:* • shows competence in subject area by using *several* strategies that develop fiction (such as dialogue, pacing, establishing point of view)	*The writing:* • establishes a situation by setting action in an understandable context • main characters are well developed • presents a conflict • has a logical plot • presents a thought-out ending	*The writing:* • is full of significant details • consistently establishes and maintains a point of view • has appropriate dialogue • is realistic • is fluent • is well organized
5 • shows competence in subject area by using *several* strategies that develop fiction	• establishes a situation by setting action in an understandable context • develops the main characters • presents a conflict • has a logical plot • presents a definite ending	• is detailed • consistently establishes and maintains a point of view • is fluent • is well paced • has appropriate dialogue

A General Fiction Rubric (cont.)

	CONTENT KNOWLEDGE	CRITICAL-THINKING PROCESSES	COMMUNICATION SKILLS
		CHECKS FOR UNDERSTANDING	
	Theme or main topic	Development of situation and characters through synthesis of ideas	Narrative aspects and strategies
4	*The writing:* • shows competence in subject area by using *some* strategies that develop fiction	*The writing:* • establishes a situation by setting action in an understandable context, but not as clearly as a 5 or 6 score • main characters are established and developed • presents a conflict • has a logical plot • has a rushed ending	*The writing:* • consistently establishes and maintains a point of view • is fluent • is well paced • has appropriate dialogue • often summarizes instead of giving details
3	• shows competence in subject area by using *some* strategies that develop fiction	• may fail to establish all elements of a story: situation, setting, main characters, conflict • may have a contrived ending	• somewhat consistently establishes a point of view • is well paced • has inappropriate dialogue
2	• shows some competence in subject area by using a *few* strategies that develop fiction	• is ineffective • shows minimal context for • doesn't develop main characters • may lack other story elements • has inconsistent characterization	• is seldom consistent • may establish a point of view • has inappropriate dialogue • is repetitive—uses several sentences with "and then"
1	• shows some competence in subject area by using a *few* strategies that develop fiction	• fails to establish context • may lack elements of a story • may stop without an ending	• is not consistent • may not have a point of view • is undeveloped or rambling • is not detailed
0	• shows no attempt	• shows no attempt	• shows no attempt

Problem Solving

Two formats for problem-solving writing

Writing English essays and writing for mathematics classes generally result in different writing styles. One standard for essay writing is *speculation about causes and effects.* Given a specific event, the writer predicts possible causes or outcomes of a given situation or experiment. Speculations can range from wild guesses to predictions based on previous experience and data.

Thinking strategies assessed in problem-solving writing

- Recognizing a problem using a variety of sources and synthesizing information
- Clarifying terms and issues
- Making generalizations

A General Problem-solving Rubric			
GENERAL AREA OF ASSESSMENT			
CONCEPTUAL UNDERSTANDING	CONTENT KNOWLEDGE	CRITICAL-THINKING PROCESSES	COMMUNICATION SKILLS
CHECKS FOR UNDERSTANDING			
Elaboration of argument	Presenting the situation	Logic and relevance of causes and effects	Coherent expression
6 *The writing:* • gives relevant and convincing evidence • substantially elaborates causes and effects • uses several strategies to support causes and effects: facts, opinions, personal experiences, specific examples	*The writing:* • clearly defines, identifies, or describes the situation • acknowledges audience's point of view • consistently demonstrates broad knowledge and understanding	*The writing:* • shows that causes or effects are clearly related to situation • uses convincing argument to convince reader of the logic of speculation • uses strategies of speculation, such as what ifs • shows direct and logical connections	*The writing:* • is in concrete language • is rich in sensory detail • is full of narrative and descriptive strategies • is aware of audience • is well organized

A General Problem-solving Rubric (cont.)

	CONCEPTUAL UNDERSTANDING	CONTENT KNOWLEDGE	CRITICAL-THINKING PROCESSES	COMMUNICATION SKILLS
	CHECKS FOR UNDERSTANDING			
	Elaboration of argument	Presenting the situation	Logic and relevance of causes and effects	Coherent expression
5	*The writing:* • gives relevant and convincing evidence • may mention several causes or effects but only elaborates on one	*The writing:* • clearly defines situation • acknowledges audience's point of view • consistently demonstrates broad knowledge and understanding	*The writing:* • shows that causes and effects are clearly related to situation • persuades • has direction and purpose • may use strategies	*The writing:* • same as a 6 score
4	• gives relevant and convincing evidence • may mention several causes or effects but only elaborates on one • may give irrelevant details	• identifies situation adequately • may have situation dominate the essay • may restate the prompt • demonstrates understanding	• establishes a connection between speculation and causes or effects • may not maintain connection	• is expressed well • may show an awareness of audience • is well organized
3	• gives limited elaboration of evidence • explains briefly one cause or effect	• presents the situation but may not demonstrate full understanding • may restate the prompt	• has speculation that is obvious or superficial • may list a series of causes and effects • may develop one cause of effect	• does not always show an awareness of audience • is organized • may lack consistency • may meander

A General Problem-solving Rubric (cont.)

	GENERAL AREA OF ASSESSMENT			
	CONCEPTUAL UNDERSTANDING	CONTENT KNOWLEDGE	CRITICAL-THINKING PROCESSES	COMMUNICATION SKILLS
	CHECKS FOR UNDERSTANDING			
	Elaboration of argument	Presenting the situation	Logic and relevance of causes and effects	Coherent expression
2	*The writing:* • shows little elaboration of evidence; may just list • may give details irrelevant and unconnected to situation	*The writing:* • shows minimal understanding of situation • may restate the prompt	*The writing:* • has speculation that is brief, meandering, and unfocused • shows little connection between speculation and causes or effects • may give causes and effects unrelated to speculation	*The writing:* • does not show an awareness of audience • is illogically organized
1	• has little or no elaboration of evidence • has little or no speculation	• develops the situation briefly or not at all	• has speculation that is brief, meandering, and unfocused • may show no logical connection between speculation and causes and effects	• does not show an awareness of audience • is poorly organized • is brief • is often incoherent
0	• shows no attempt	• shows no attempt	• shows no attempt	• shows no attempt

For mathematics classes and the like, problem-solving writing may require hypothesizing, designing an experiment, or solving a mathematical problem.

A General Mathematics Rubric[4]			
GENERAL AREA OF ASSESSMENT			
CONCEPTUAL UNDERSTANDING	CONTENT KNOWLEDGE	CRITICAL-THINKING PROCESSES	COMMUNICATION SKILLS
CHECKS FOR UNDERSTANDING			
Controlling idea	Mathematical information	Problem solving	Text, diagrams, charts, and drawings
6 *The writing:* • shows understanding of open-ended problem, math ideas, and processes	*The writing:* • has clear and simple diagrams • includes examples	*The writing:* • identifies all the important elements of the problem • presents strong supporting arguments	*The writing:* • is clear • is coherent • is unambiguous • is complete in its explanation
5 • shows understanding of open-ended problem, math ideas, and processes	• has clear and simple diagrams • includes examples	• identifies the most important elements of the problem • presents solid supporting arguments	• is clear • is coherent • is unambiguous • is complete in its explanation
4 • shows understanding of open-ended problem, math ideas, and processes	• has a diagram that may be inappropriate or unclear	• identifies the most important elements of the problem • may present an incomplete argument	• is clear • is coherent • is unambiguous • is not clear in its explanation
3 • fails to show full understanding of math ideas and processes	• makes computational errors • has a diagram that may be inappropriate or unclear	• identifies some elements of the problem • may have weak arguments	• reflects an inappropriate strategy for solving the problem

A General Mathematics Rubric (cont.)

	CONCEPTUAL UNDERSTANDING	CONTENT KNOWLEDGE	CRITICAL-THINKING PROCESSES	COMMUNICATION SKILLS
	CHECKS FOR UNDERSTANDING			
	Controlling idea	Mathematical information	Problem solving	Text, diagrams, charts, and drawings
2	*The writing:* • shows no understanding	*The writing:* • makes computational errors • has a diagram that may be inappropriate or unclear	*The writing:* • identifies few elements of the problem • gives no support	*The writing:* • is not understandable
1	• shows no understanding	• has a diagram that may be inappropriate or unclear	• copies from question	• is not understandable
0	• shows no attempt	• shows no attempt	• shows no attempt	• shows no attempt

Exercise: Develop Your Own Rubric

1. Write your open-ended question.

2. Copy the related generic rubric matrix or use it as a guideline.

3. Answer each question for the different general assessment areas from the generic rubric on page 23.

4. Decide what areas of assessment are appropriate for your specific open-ended question.

5. Choose the number of achievement levels you wish to have for this rubric.

6. List the characteristics needed for each achievement level in each assessment area. Use the many samples in this chapter for ideas.

7. Assign each achievement level a grade or point value.

Presenting Open-ended Questions to Students: A Model

Before students can answer open-ended questions successfully, they must understand the vocabulary used in the different questioning formats. Students' frustration with essays isn't always from lack of content knowledge, but from not understanding the vocabulary used in the question. This chapter presents one method to introduce your students to the open-ended questioning format.

Answering open-ended questions may take longer than using traditional assessment methods. Plan to use open-ended questions instead of some of your other testing techniques. Remember that open-ended questions can take as little as fifteen minutes or as long as a couple of days.

As you walk your students through sample questions, plan extra time for them to work on their responses. You may want to spend a day or two preparing your students for future questions. Make sure they understand the vocabulary and directions for answering open-ended questions.

Here's one model for student success:

1. The First Day

Take ten to fifteen minutes of class, when convenient, to introduce open-ended questions. Remind students that part of assessment is the ability to communicate in writing. Pass out a sample question (use the one on page 45, or prepare your own). Read the question aloud, and have students interpret each sentence

Many students reported that they did not understand the meaning of such terms as relevance, bias, consistency, stereotype and evidence. Students who lacked a critical thinking vocabulary were unable to describe the steps and strategies they used during problem solving.

Jan Talbot,
Social Studies Consultant[1]

and underline the directions. Answer any vocabulary questions the students have. Provide time in your lessons for interpreting the specific vocabulary for different questioning formats.

Students should gather information and write a rough-draft response as class work or homework. Tell students to pause about three-fourths of the way through their writing, re-read the directions, and check to see if they are still on track.

2. *The Second Day*

Share your grading rubric or develop one with your class. Have students, in pairs, read each other's rough drafts with the rubric in mind. Tell them to exchange ideas for improving papers. Students should rewrite their papers, incorporating the suggestions from the peer review and researching further if necessary.

3. *The Third Day*

Quickly check students' rough drafts for content understanding. Conduct a class discussion of some of the misconceptions you find. Then ask students to review their research materials and produce their final draft.

4. *Grading*

Grade according to your developed rubric. Accept rough drafts and other notes for partial credit. Let students know ahead of time the point values you have assigned for each part of their response.

You might want to use this model to present your first few questions. Then, students should be able to follow directions for writing with one quick reading. They can often finish their responses in one class period. Each time you present an open-ended question, read the question aloud and determine how well your students understand it. Encourage students to underline the directions for writing. They should refer to the directions often as they write rough and final drafts.

Sample Question

This open-ended question follows the descriptive questioning format. The situation and directions for writing are combined in this example. Directions for writing are underlined.

When in This World?

Scientists have divided earth's history into four major eras: Pre-Cambrian, Paleozoic, Cenozoic, and Mesozoic. Using your research information and classroom experiences, choose one era and <u>describe it.</u> Don't forget to <u>include the biological and physical changes</u> in the environment that affected life during that time. <u>Include the major events</u> that determined the beginning and end of the era you choose.

Possible student interpretations of the question

- Sentence one is a statement of facts.
- Sentence two asks the writer to do something using research and classroom information.
- Sentences three and four give more information and directions as to what to include in writing. They help the writer focus.

Possible steps in completing a first draft

These ideas should come from students as they interpret the question.

- Choose one era to write about.
- Gather research information and classroom notes.
- Identify special events that designated the beginning and end of this era.
- Separate biological changes from physical changes to the environment.
- Read through notes.
- Write rough draft.

When in This World?		
GENERAL AREA OF ASSESSMENT		
CONCEPTUAL UNDERSTANDING	CONTENT KNOWLEDGE	CRITICAL-THINKING PROCESSES
CHECKS FOR UNDERSTANDING		
• classifies eras of historical time by specific physical and biological factors	• demonstrates physical and biological characteristics for each geological era	• shows ability to group, organize, and explain

The complete rubric would be followed by point levels and the corresponding breakdown of the checks for understanding.

Sample Open-ended Questions with Rubrics

This chapter contains eighteen sample questions in various questioning formats and curricular areas, including mathematics, social science, science, and language arts. A simple rubric follows each question. You should assume students have already studied the concepts being assessed in the question. Use these examples with your students or adapt them to your specific needs.

Curricular area: mathematics
Questioning format: problem solving

Write Your Own Problem[1]

Write a brief math story that can be represented by the following statement:

$$2n + 4 = 20$$

Directions for writing:

1. *Define the problem. Write clearly enough so that someone picking up your paper could understand exactly what you were asked to do.*

2. *Discuss your method of solving the problem. What did you try? What worked? What didn't work? How did you get started? What did you do when you got stuck? How*

many different approaches did you try? Did you talk to anyone about the problem? Did that help or hinder you?

3. *Review your process. How do you know your story fits the equation? What did you learn about mathematics? What did you learn about yourself? Was the problem too easy, too hard, or just right?*

Write Your Own Problem		
GENERAL AREA OF ASSESSMENT		
CONCEPTUAL UNDERSTANDING	CONTENT KNOWLEDGE	CRITICAL-THINKING PROCESSES
CHECKS FOR UNDERSTANDING		
• writes word problems	• interprets mathematical equations	• synthesizes

Curricular area: mathematics

Questioning format: problem solving

A Paper-Folding Problem

There once was a famous Japanese paper folder—a master of origami. He could make almost anything by intricately folding square pieces of paper: frogs, cranes, deer, and even people. Unfortunately, this paper folder was not good at mathematics, and it nearly cost him his life savings.

One day a stranger came to the paper folder. "I have a simple paper-folding problem," he said. "I will bet you ten thousand yen that you cannot solve it."

Of course, the paper folder accepted the bet because he could fold paper better than anyone in the world. Here was the problem:

*Take a square sheet of paper. Fold it in half. Fold it in half
again . . . again . . . and again. Continue until you have
folded the paper in half 25 times. How many thicknesses of
paper are there in the folded paper?*

*The paper folder tried several times, but couldn't solve the
problem. Why not? Help him by finding what the thickness
of the paper would be after 25 folds. (Express your answer in
the largest possible units.)*

Directions for writing:

1. *Define the problem. Write clearly enough so that someone
   reading your paper could understand exactly what you
   were asked to do.*

2. *Discuss your method of solving the paper folder's problem.
   What did you try? What worked? What didn't work? How
   did you get started? What did you do when you got stuck?
   How many different approaches did you try? Did you talk
   to anyone about the problem? Did that help or hinder
   you?*

3. *Review your process. What answer did you get? What
   makes you think you got it right? What did you learn
   about mathematics? What did you learn about yourself?
   Was the problem too easy, too hard, or just right?*

A Paper-Folding Problem			
GENERAL AREA OF ASSESSMENT			
CONCEPTUAL UNDERSTANDING	CONTENT KNOWLEDGE	CRITICAL-THINKING PROCESSES	COMMUNICATION SKILLS
SPECIFIC CHECKS FOR UNDERSTANDING			
• uses exponents	• understands powers of 2	• analyzes, problem solves	• interprets word problems

Curricular area: mathematics
Questioning format: problem solving

Wright Wheels Inventory

Orville and Wilbur own a bicycle shop that also sells tricycles. One day they took an inventory. They each counted one type of item, which would have worked fine if one had counted bicycles and the other had counted tricycles. But Orville counted the number of pedals in the shop, and Wilbur counted the wheels. They counted 144 pedals and 186 wheels. All pedals and wheels were parts of either bicycles or tricycles. They were about to start over when their friend Kitty challenged them to figure out the number of bicycles and tricycles from the information they had. Can you help them? Directions for writing:

1. *Define the problem. Write clearly enough so that someone reading your paper could understand exactly what you were asked to do.*

2. *Discuss your method of solving the problem. What did you try? What worked? What didn't work? How did you get started? What did you do when you got stuck? How many different approaches did you try? Did you talk to anyone about the problem? Did that help or hinder you?*

3. *Review your process. What answer did you get? What makes you think you got it right? What did you learn about mathematics? What did you learn about yourself?*

Wright Wheels Inventory		
GENERAL AREA OF ASSESSMENT		
CONCEPTUAL UNDERSTANDING	CONTENT KNOWLEDGE	CRITICAL-THINKING PROCESSES
CHECKS FOR UNDERSTANDING		
• uses variables	• writes and solves simultaneous equations	• problem solves

Curricular area: mathematics

Questioning format: description

Banners in a Hurry[2]

You are in charge of getting the banners for your upcoming geometry awards ceremony. You have pictures you want printed on the banners. You try to FAX the pictures to the print shop, but find out their FAX is broken, so you will have to call in your order.

Directions for writing: Write out the set of directions you will give the print shop over the phone so they will make two banners that look exactly like the figures below.

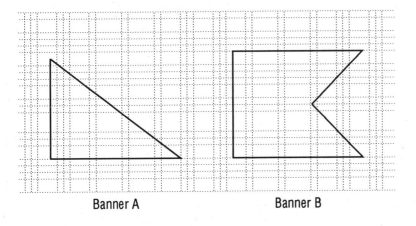

Banner A   Banner B

Banners in a Hurry		
GENERAL AREA OF ASSESSMENT		
CONCEPTUAL UNDERSTANDING	CONTENT KNOWLEDGE	CRITICAL-THINKING PROCESSES
CHECKS FOR UNDERSTANDING		
• understands geometric shapes	• effectively uses terminology and knowledge of coordinate geometry	• describes and orders information

Curricular area: history/social sciences
Questioning format: evaluation

Space, Politics, and Money

You've just joined the debating team at your high school. The debate issue is this: Could the money spent from 1960 to 1990 for the United States space program have been better spent solving domestic problems? As a team, brainstorm ideas for this topic, conduct research, and determine your team's stance.

Directions for writing: With your group, brainstorm, research, and choose a stance. Then, on your own, write an essay defending your position. Your essay will differ from your teammates' essays. As you brainstorm, keep in mind politics, social priorities, domestic issues, and the technological benefits and detriments of the space program.

Space, Politics, and Money		
GENERAL AREA OF ASSESSMENT		
CONCEPTUAL UNDERSTANDING	CONTENT KNOWLEDGE	CRITICAL-THINKING PROCESSES
CHECKS FOR UNDERSTANDING		
• understands government spending and priorities	• knows about specific benefits derived from the space program, nationalism, cost of both, and domestic issues including housing, jobs, health, and pollution	• evaluates

Curricular area: history/social sciences
Questioning format: fiction

Capturing the Crusades

You are a twelve-year-old page to a knight during the Crusades. You've left Italy with the latest group of crusaders heading for the Holy Lands. You are an active observer of what is happening around you. During the trip, you write in a diary to describe your job, the sights you see, and the troubles you encounter.

Directions for writing: Write a set of diary entries as if you were traveling with a group of crusaders. The entries may include, but are not limited to, the duties of your job, what it is like to travel on foot, the boat ride to Acra, and the hardships you endure. You can describe your first day in Acra and/or tell about meeting a Muslim your age at a watering hole and sharing a meal.

Capturing the Crusades		
GENERAL AREA OF ASSESSMENT		
CONCEPTUAL UNDERSTANDING	CONTENT KNOWLEDGE	CRITICAL-THINKING PROCESSES
CHECKS FOR UNDERSTANDING		
• understands the Crusades	• is familiar with the duties of a servant or page in the Middle Ages, trade routes to the Middle East, life in Acra, lifestyles of Europeans traveling on Crusade during the Middle Ages, Muslim culture	• synthesizes and fictionalizes

Curricular area: history/social sciences
Questioning format: problem solving

South Versus North, Again

Your cousin from Alabama sent you another newspaper clipping speculating about what the United States would have been like if the South had won the Civil War. It gets you thinking. A lot of things happened after the war ended. What would have changed if the South had won?

Directions for writing: Describe how the United States would have been different if the South had won the Civil War. Focus on the first twenty-five years after the war. Speculate on what the government would have been like. Use reasons and evidence to support your position. Use the following questions as guidelines: What did the North and South stand for on social, political, and economic issues? How might the westward movement have been affected? What would have happened to the industrialization of the North and West?

South Versus North, Again		
GENERAL AREA OF ASSESSMENT		
CONCEPTUAL UNDERSTANDING	CONTENT KNOWLEDGE	CRITICAL-THINKING PROCESSES
CHECKS FOR UNDERSTANDING		
• knows about the American Civil War	• has in-depth knowledge of the issues surrounding the Civil War, including slavery, states' rights, tariffs, and federal money for transportation	• problem solves, and speculates about causes and effects

Curricular area: history/social sciences
Questioning format: description

Moving West

You are a working-class young adult living in New York around 1850. Some of your friends have decided to move west. You've heard about the hardship, dangers, and rewards of going westward. You have promised your friends you will write them to give your decision.

Directions for writing: Think about your study of the westward movement. Decide whether or not you would go. Write a letter to your friends describing your reasons.

Moving West		
GENERAL AREA OF ASSESSMENT		
CONCEPTUAL UNDERSTANDING	CONTENT KNOWLEDGE	CRITICAL-THINKING PROCESSES
CHECKS FOR UNDERSTANDING		
• understands the westward movement	• knows the dangers: attack by travelers or Native Americans; sickness; starvation; accidents; childbirth; lack of water • knows the hardships: preparing supplies; weather; difficult trails; forming relationships; making repairs • knows the rewards: relationships; better opportunities; land strength of character; independence	• describes the dangers, hardships, and rewards

Curricular area: earth science
Questioning format: description

Crystals Revealed by Network Specialist

Imagine that you are a crystal specialist. You are often sent on unusual assignments, but none of them compare to the assignment you received today. Thanks to an advancement in electron microscopy technology, you will be "miniaturized"—placed inside a crystal! Your job will be to walk through the crystal, describing what you see.

Directions for writing: You may choose a crystal from any of the six crystal systems studied in class. Write a narrative of what you see inside one crystal from a molecular point of view. Include all you can about the external and internal structure of the crystal. What physical properties does the crystal have because of its molecular structure? What other observations can you make while you are miniaturized? Use diagrams if it will enhance your description. Remember, this is headline news!

Crystals Revealed by Network Specialist			
GENERAL AREA OF ASSESSMENT			
CONCEPTUAL UNDERSTANDING	CONTENT KNOWLEDGE	CRITICAL-THINKING PROCESSES	COMMUNICATION SKILLS
CHECKS FOR UNDERSTANDING			
• understands crystal formation	• understands axial lines, cleavage, bonding, molecular structure, and physical properties	• synthesizes information, groups, and sorts	• describes and reports information

Curricular area: ecology
Questioning format: evaluation

Antarctica—You Make the Call

You are heading a Research Task Force that will determine whether or how Antarctica will be developed. Your expedition will leave in one month. Design a plan that will help you make the best recommendation on the future use of Antarctica.

Directions for writing: As you write your report with your recommendation on whether and how Antarctica should be developed, ponder these questions: What will you take? Who will you take with you? What research will you do before you go and while you are there? Who will help you make your decision?

Antarctica—You Make the Call		
GENERAL AREA OF ASSESSMENT		
CONCEPTUAL UNDERSTANDING	CONTENT KNOWLEDGE	CRITICAL-THINKING PROCESSES
CHECKS FOR UNDERSTANDING		
• understands ecological relationships as they refer to the isolated Antarctica	• knows what tests to make to study ecological relationships and how to find minerals and other natural resources • knows the different science fields involved in studying ecosystems	• evaluates and synthesizes information

Curricular area: chemistry
Questioning format: evaluation

Lunch at the Top

Your family has started their annual summer trek to your cousin's home in Colorado. As usual, you are in charge of cooking. You reach the continental divide, elevation approximately 11,000 feet (5,200 meters) at lunch time. Everyone asks for boiled egg sandwiches, saying that you can boil the eggs faster at higher elevations.

Directions for writing: Write an informative paper about boiling water at higher elevations. Is atmospheric pressure lower at higher elevations? What causes boiling to take place? How does temperature affect the rate of a chemical reaction, such as boiling an egg? What chemical and physical processes affect your ability to prepare lunch?[3]

Lunch at the Top		
GENERAL AREA OF ASSESSMENT		
CONCEPTUAL UNDERSTANDING	CONTENT KNOWLEDGE	CRITICAL-THINKING PROCESSES
CHECKS FOR UNDERSTANDING		
• understands how physical properties of the atmosphere affect chemical reactions	• understands atmospheric pressure; heat; chemical reactions; and temperature	• evaluates and synthesizes processes information

Curricular area: physical science
Questioning format: fiction

As Rays Go

Pretend you are energy that originated at the sun's surface. You leave the sun's surface and travel through space toward earth.

Directions for writing: Write a story about what might happen to you as you travel through space, arrive at earth's atmosphere, maybe reach the surface of the earth, and perhaps even get absorbed by one of the experiments the class put outside in the last two weeks. Describe your journey. Where do you finally come to rest, or do you?

As Rays Go		
GENERAL AREA OF ASSESSMENT		
CONCEPTUAL UNDERSTANDING	CONTENT KNOWLEDGE	CRITICAL-THINKING PROCESSES
CHECKS FOR UNDERSTANDING		
• understands that energy travels as waves and that the radiant energy from the sun is transformed	• understands electromagnetic spectrum, waves, rays, radiation, conduction, heat, temperature, absorption, reflection, and refraction	• fictionalizes and synthesizes information

Curricular area: English/language arts
Questioning format: problem solving

Double Endings

*Imagine you are the author of*_____ [the title of a story or novel; choose the point during the reading at which this question will be appropriate] *and have written the story or novel up to this point. You are considering several possible endings for the novel. Write a letter to your publisher, who has read what you've written so far. In your letter, briefly describe two possible endings, and speculate about how each might be appropriate given what you have already written.*

Directions for writing: Give details of plot, actions, and character from the already-written part of your novel. Mention the advantages and disadvantages of each ending. Compare them and speculate which would be best. Remember to support your speculations with reasons and evidence. Convince your publisher to choose the ending you think would be best.

Double Endings		
GENERAL AREA OF ASSESSMENT		
CONCEPTUAL UNDERSTANDING	CONTENT KNOWLEDGE	CRITICAL-THINKING PROCESSES
CHECKS FOR UNDERSTANDING		
• understands that after carefully analyzing an author's style, alternative endings may be written	• formats an argument with logical sequencing of events	• problem solves, and speculates about causes and effects

Curricular area: English/language arts
Questioning format: evaluation

Poetry in Motion

You have just finished a unit on reading and analyzing poetry. Now it is time to compile a book called Ten Best Poems for the Eighth Grade.

Directions for writing: Pick your favorite poem from the poems you have read. Write an evaluation for the review board, which will be composed of students, teachers, and parents who have read the poem. Convince the review board that the poem you have chosen should be included in the collection of poems for eighth-grade students. Give reasons why, and give specific evidence from the poem to support your reasons.

Poetry in Motion		
GENERAL AREA OF ASSESSMENT		
CONCEPTUAL UNDERSTANDING	CONTENT KNOWLEDGE	CRITICAL-THINKING PROCESSES
CHECKS FOR UNDERSTANDING		
• shows understanding of poetic forms	• reads and understands poetry • knows the elements of poetry	• evaluates, makes a judgment, and writes reasons and evidence

Curricular area: English/language arts
Questioning format: problem solving

Tom Sawyer in Trouble Again

Tom and Becky are lost and have been trapped in the cave for some time. Before reading the next chapter in the book, propose a solution to their dilemma.

Directions for writing: Write a solution to Tom and Becky's dilemma. How will they get out of the cave? What will they do about their unexpected meeting with Injun Joe? What will they eat? How will they see? How will they find a way out? Or will they? Support your solution with evidence from what you already know about the characters and their actions.

Tom Sawyer in Trouble Again		
GENERAL AREA OF ASSESSMENT		
CONCEPTUAL UNDERSTANDING	CONTENT KNOWLEDGE	CRITICAL-THINKING PROCESSES
CHECKS FOR UNDERSTANDING		
• knows Tom Sawyer	• gives specific details from the novel • analyzes characters and predicts their behaviors	• problem solves

Curricular area: English/language arts
Questioning format: problem solving

Fads on Campus[3]

*You may have noticed fads of some sort at school. A **fad** is a custom or style that people are very interested in for a short time. Many fads have to do with appearance (clothing, jewelry, or hair styles) or with speech (certain words or phrases that everyone uses). Perhaps you can think of other kinds of fads.*

Directions for writing: Choose a fad you have observed at school. Write an essay describing this fad, and analyze what caused it. Do not be satisfied with describing just the most obvious cause, because fads usually have several causes. Remember, you are writing this essay for your teacher, who might enjoy learning about a current fad at school and what caused it. Convince your teacher that your proposed causes may actually explain why the fad appeared.

Fads on Campus		
GENERAL AREA OF ASSESSMENT		
CONCEPTUAL UNDERSTANDING	CONTENT KNOWLEDGE	CRITICAL-THINKING PROCESSES
CHECKS FOR UNDERSTANDING		
• reasons and evidence	• speculates about the causes of a situation • identifies several causes	• speculates about causes and solves problems

Curricular area: cross-curricular/other
Questioning format: analysis

A Play for AIDS

You are writing a play about AIDS for a middle school audience. But first, you need to persuade the Arts committee to fund your project. Get together with your three best playwright buddies and brainstorm ideas on what you will do.

Directions for writing: After brainstorming with your colleagues, each of you should write your own proposal to the committee. Your proposal should be no longer than three pages. Keep in mind these questions: What are the social issues of presenting a play on AIDS? Will your play be a comedy, musical, or drama? How will you get across the mathematics of how the disease spreads? What will be the best way to present the science behind AIDS? Will you allow the audience to ask questions? What sort of preview information will you present to the administration of the schools where you plan to present the play?

A Play for AIDS			
GENERAL AREA OF ASSESSMENT			
CONCEPTUAL UNDERSTANDING	CONTENT KNOWLEDGE	CRITICAL-THINKING PROCESSES	COMMUNICATION SKILLS
CHECKS FOR UNDERSTANDING			
• understands that AIDS is a disease that crosses political, social, and moral boundaries	• knows statistics of how the disease spreads and the science behind AIDS • understands some of the social implications	• synthesizes and applies knowledge • makes decisions	• writes persuasively

Curricular area: cross-curricular

Questioning format: comparison

Different Time, Different Plague

Compare the London Bubonic Plagues of the 1600s to the AIDS epidemic.

Directions for writing: Write a comparison about these two diseases. Keep in mind how the government acted and acts in regard to treatment, prevention, research, and transmission of the diseases. What were and are the social responses? For example, how did and do people treat carriers? What sort of education did and do we have about each disease? How did and does lifestyle affect the possibility of contracting either disease? How many people died or are dying? What were or are the chances of you getting either disease?

Different Time, Different Plague		
GENERAL AREA OF ASSESSMENT		
CONCEPTUAL UNDERSTANDING	CONTENT KNOWLEDGE	CRITICAL-THINKING PROCESSES
CHECKS FOR UNDERSTANDING		
• understands plagues and some ways of dealing with them	• understands the social issues, science, and mathematical spread of both diseases	• compares issues

Putting It Together: An Example of the Process

In this chapter you will examine the process, from developing the question to reading the student responses, in an actual classroom example.

Assume that you have just ended a unit on interacting environmental systems. The unit focused on the forces that cause change and create features on the earth's surface.

You plan to give a open-ended question take-home exam, asking your students to summarize their conceptual knowledge from the unit. You teach middle school students, so you will name several key concepts in the prompt. (For less or more sophisticated students, the conceptual details would vary.)

Writing the Question

For this question, you decide to assess your students' knowledge of the role plate tectonics play in forming many of the earth's features. The concept being assessed is that plate tectonics is responsible for the features of the surface of the earth; the subconcepts are sea-floor spreading, plate boundary movements, and features on the earth's surface. The critical-thinking processes you assess in this question are synthesizing information and making generalizations. You will use the fiction questioning format.

You write a question situation that sets the student in a story-teller role. Students are to imagine themselves as indestructible beings that meander through earth's crust and mantle. Your directions for writing include a summary of the work students did in their laboratory experiments, research, and model making.

Your rubric includes the concepts and content knowledge taught in the unit. The fiction questioning format provides the critical-thinking processes and communication skills criteria for the rubric. You decide to have three separate levels of achievement.

Forces of the Earth

Imagine you are an indestructible being that can wander under, through, and over the earth's crust. You decide to write a story about some of your journeys, telling about the earth's changes from your unique perspective.

Directions for writing: This science unit focused on how the forces of the earth change and shape the physical features of the earth's surface. You've studied physical forces, such as plate tectonics, convection, buoyancy, and density. You've observed, studied, and made models of sea-floor spreading, magnetic reversals, and plate boundary movements. You've researched undersea features and land features such as volcanoes, earthquakes, ridges, mountains, and trenches. You've played the roles of an oceanographer, a map maker, and others in your projects.

Write a story that tells of a journey inside and outside the surface of the earth. Start "anywhere" and "anywhen" in earth's geological history, and trace your path as you move around in the mantle and the crust. Describe your journey as you become molten in the mantle. Do you become a part of one of the many plates? Do you become a part of the process of an undersea mountain that will someday be the newest Hawaiian island? Do you spend time at the Mid-Atlantic range?

Presenting the Question

You give the Forces of the Earth question as a take-home exam, allowing the students three days to compose, write, edit, and rewrite. The students can use notes, research materials, the library, and class laboratory work during this time. You confer with those who ask. Students check their own papers for grammar and punctuation. Several write more than one draft during the time allotted. You decide to critique drafts before final work is to be handed in.

When the final papers are turned in, you notice that students focused mostly on the process of undersea volcanic activity. Some drew pictures to accompany their writing. Here are three samples of student writing.

Sample one

"I had just settled down for a short nap among my fiery friends when I was suddenly jolted awake. I felt myself slowly rising to the surface. At first I was annoyed at having been woken up, but then I forgot my annoyance and became excited. I had never seen the earth's crust or surface. I'd always been stuck down in the mantle.

So anyhow, I finally reached the top of the earth's crust and came spilling out the top of a volcano. I heard some weird two-legged beings screaming about a ring of fire (I found out later that these beings were "hewmans" or something like that). I would have liked to have listened to these hewmans longer, but I had other matters to deal with. For, to my horror, I realized that I was being stretched out all down the mountain. And not only that, but I was hardening! It was awful.

Well, I decided to just stay where I was, and wait for something else to happen (actually, I didn't have much choice, being hardened and all). And sure enough after just a decade or two of waiting, I felt the earth shaking beneath me. My first thought was, "Cool, something's finally happening!" but not for long.

Open-ended questions allow students to demonstrate the depth of their understanding of a problem, almost an impossibility with multiple-choice items.

California Assessment Program[1]

For after a few seconds I felt half of me being pulled one way, and the other half being pulled the other way. It was a terrible feeling. And then, suddenly, I just snapped in two. I (we?) felt awful.

I just sat there feeling sorry for myself for a few years, and I probably would have for a lot longer, but then up the mountain came some hewmans and they started picking at me with great big metal things and breaking little pieces off of me. And then they picked these pieces up, threw them in a bag, and walked away with them. I was furious. But there was nothing I could do about it. I cursed my ill luck of being hardened and unable to move freely like I used to. And then, just to rub it in, one of the hewmans said that I was very dense and that I would probably stink (or did he say sink?). I was insulted. "I'm very intelligent!" I wanted to yell out, but of course I couldn't. All I could do was sit there. And here I am still. I wonder what will happen to me next . . ."

Teacher comments: The student's use of humor enhances the demonstrated scientific understanding. While specifics are not spelled out, it is obvious the student understood the scientific concepts and synthesized them into a story.

Sample two

"Bubble, Bubble, pop!" I am a great hot mass of bubbling boiling liquid hotter than any other material substance on earth. I am very powerful. I live within the very center of the enormous earth. I am MOLTEN!

I swirl around for thousands of years inside mother earth and then the day comes when I am surrounded by so much pressure that I burst through the outer layers of the earth. I crash through the mantle then blast out of the top of an underwater volcano into the cold wrath of the undersea. Part of me dies because of the cold water, but another part of me bursts out into the clear air and I form a volcano island.

I settle back down and every few thousand years the

pressure once again builds up and I burst out onto the earth with excitement.

Over the millions of years I have lived I see many changes in the earth's plates. And every time I venture to the surface the continents of the earth have shifted. Over the years I also see civilization develop and new structures and beings all over the planet.

I am now very old and the earth is taking a large turn. Pollution from factories and machines is devastating the worlds' living things. If this keeps up the earth will not live to see the next millennium. This tragic turn of pollution taking over can not be stopped by any one, but needs an effort from beings world wide. This is my last visit in the outside world because I am cooling off and dying out. "Goodbye world, fight for your life and live a long and plentiful life."

Teacher comments: While this student's scientific understanding is not entirely accurate, the language style is delightful. The student even included a moral commentary on pollution.

Sample three

Hello my name is Crustor I live forever I am going to take a trip through the earth I will start in the Atlantic ocean I dive into the ocean and go to the bottom of the sear floor where I encounter an underwater volcano I dive right through it into the molten lava it is strange because rocks in the lava are coming at me right and left I finally break into the earth's crust, a very hard surface that I have entered my trip is very bumpy but all the sudden I am gliding in the mantles molten It somewhat nice the underwater volcano then I start my journey back the other way I mainly hit all the same spots on my way in except when I come up on the sea I see a continental shelf and slope and a hot spot I have enjoyed my journey and will take it again sometime.

Teacher comments: The reference to the Atlantic ocean reflected earlier class work. The student neglected punctuation, but showed an understanding of convection and movement inside the earth.

The act of writing is an act of thought.

Donald Murray,
Professor English[2]

Assessing the Essays

Most students focused only on how volcanoes are formed, and not on other surface features as had been expected. After reading the essays, you adjust the rubric to reflect the responses that were elicited and to be able to grade accordingly. You also rephrase the question for future exams to encourage responses that more broadly reflect the concepts presented in the unit.

You decide to grade this question holistically. First, you read the papers once and divide them into three categories according to conceptual and content understanding. Then you re-scan for critical-thinking processes and communication skills. Since this is the first time you've asked students this question, you use the rubric as a guideline and note modifications you will make for future exams. You keep samples of your students' responses to use as benchmarks.

Forces of the Earth			
GENERAL AREA OF ASSESSMENT			
CONCEPTUAL UNDERSTANDING	CONTENT KNOWLEDGE	CRITICAL-THINKING PROCESSES	COMMUNICATION SKILLS
CHECKS FOR UNDERSTANDING			
• understands plate tectonics, convection buoyancy, and density	• knows about sea-floor spreading, plate boundary movements, and undersea and land volcanoes	• synthesizes • makes generalizations • describes • compares	• writes with error-free grammar and good punctuation
3 — *The writing:* • demonstrates understanding of all concepts	*The writing:* • uses all areas of content	*The writing:* • shows ability to synthesize concepts together • fits generalization with conceptual understanding • describes and compares completely and with relevance to generalization	*The writing:* • has only one or two errors in grammar and punctuation

Forces of the Earth (cont.)

	CONCEPTUAL UNDERSTANDING	CONTENT KNOWLEDGE	CRITICAL-THINKING PROCESSES	COMMUNICATION SKILLS
	CHECKS FOR UNDERSTANDING			
	• understands plate tectonics, convection buoyancy, and density	• knows about sea-floor spreading, plate boundary movements, and undersea and land volcanoes	• synthesizes • makes generalizations • describes • compares	• writes with error-free grammar and good punctuation
2	*The writing:* • demonstrates under-standing of two to four concepts	*The writing:* • uses several areas of content in writing • demonstrates under-standing of several content items	*The writing:* • synthesizes concepts well • generalizes fairly well • describes and compares completely and with relevance to general-ization	*The writing:* • has only a few errors in grammar and punctuation
1	• demonstrates under-standing of one to two concepts	• uses one or two areas of content in writing • demonstrates under-standing of one or two concepts	• may not synthesize concepts together • has good descriptions and comparisons • may be weak in generalization	• has many errors in grammar and punctuation
0	• made no attempt	• made no attempt	• made no attempt	• made no attempt

Notes

Chapter One

1. Linda Nott, Colleen Reeve, and Raymond Reeve, "Scoring Rubrics: An Assessment Option," *Science Scope,* March 1992, p. 44.

2. Barry K. Beyer, *Practical Strategies for the Teaching of Thinking* (Boston: Allyn and Bacon, 1987), p. 1.

3. John Chaffee, *Thinking Critically* (Boston: Houghton Mifflin, 1988), p. 26.

4. Beyer, *Practical Strategies,* p. 8.

5. Arthur Applebee, *Writing in the Secondary School: English and the Content Area* (Urbana, Ill.: National Council of Teachers of English), 1981. And James Britton, et al., *The Development of Writing Abilities* (New York: Macmillan, 1975), pp. 11–18.

6. Jan Talbot, "The Assessment of Critical Thinking in History/Social Science Through Writing," *Social Studies Review,* Winter 1986, p. 38.

Chapter Two

1. Key concepts taken from Bernard J. Nebel, *Environmental Science: The Way the World Works* (Englewood Cliffs, N.J.: Prentice Hall, 1987), p. 68.

Chapter Three

1. Peter Kneedler, "Statewide Assessment in History/Social Science Grade Eight: Why and What Happened," *Social Studies Review,* Winter 1986, Vol. 25:2, p. 10.

Chapter Four

1. Adapted from Robin L. H. Freedman, *Connections: Science by Writing* (Paradise, Calif.: Serin House Publishers, 1990), p. 4.

2. Rosemary G. Messick and Karen E. Reynolds, *Middle Level Curriculum in Action* (New York: Longman Publishing Group, 1992), p. 213.

3. David Cardwell, response from a workshop on writing and administering open-ended questions, Sacramento, April 1992.

4. Adapted from California State Department of Education, *A Question of Thinking: A First Look at Students' Performance on Open-Ended Questions in Math* (CSDE: Sacramento, 1989), p. 53.

Chapter Five

1. Talbot, "The Assessment of Critical Thinking," p. 39.

2. Inez Fugate Liftig, Bob Liftig, and Karen Eaker, "Making Assessment Work: What Teachers Should Know Before They Try It," *Science Scope,* March 1992, p. 8.

Chapter Six

1. The first three problems are adapted with permission from Joel Wells, personal communication, 1992.

2. Adapted from California State Department of Education, *Golden State Examination, GSE Chemistry* (CSDE: Sacramento, 1991), p. 7.

3. Adapted from California State Department of Education, *Writing Assessment Handbook, Grade Eight* (CSDE: Sacramento, 1990), Ch. XIII, p. 6.

Chapter Seven

1. California Assessment Program, *California: The State of Assessment* (Sacramento: California State Department of Education, 1990), p. 25.

2. Donald M. Murray, *A Writer Teaches Writing* (Boston: Houghton Mifflin Co., 1985), p. 3.

References

Applebee, Arthur. *Writing in the Secondary School: English and the Content Area*. Urbana, Ill.: National Council of Teachers of English, 1981.

Beyer, Barry K. *Practical Strategies for the Teaching of Thinking*. Boston: Allyn and Bacon, 1987.

Britton, James, et al. *The Development of Writing Abilities*. New York: Macmillan, 1975.

California Assessment Program. *California: The State of Assessment*. Sacramento: California State Department of Education, 1990.

California State Department of Education. *Golden State Examination, GSE Chemistry*. Sacramento: CSDE, 1991.

——— . *A Question of Thinking: A First Look at Students' Performance on Open-Ended Questions in Math*. CSDE: Sacramento, 1989.

——— . Student Essays *Illustrating the CAP Rhetorical Effectiveness Scoring System, Grade 12*. Sacramento: CSDE, 1989.

——— . *Writing Assessment Handbook, Grade Eight*. Sacramento: CSDE, 1990.

——— . *Writing Assessment Handbook, Grade Twelve*. Sacramento: CSDE, 1987.

California Council for the Social Studies. *Social Studies Review: California's New Statewide Assessment in History/Social Science*. Roseville, Calif.: CCSS, Winter 1986, Vol. 25, No. 2.

Chaffee, John. *Thinking Critically*. Boston: Houghton Mifflin, 1988.

Densimore, Cheryl. Personal correspondence, 1987.

Elbow, Peter. *Writing With Power: Techniques for Mastering the Writing Process*. Oxford: Oxford University Press, 1981.

Fitzgibbon, Joe. *Persona Book II*. Littleton, Mass.: Sundance Publishers and Distributors, 1985.

Fort Bragg Writing Program, Fort Bragg, Calif.: Fort Bragg Unified School District, 1986.

Freedman, Robin L. H. *Connections: Writing and Science Achievement, A Handbook for Middle/Junior High School Science Teachers*. Harrisburg, Pa.: Pennsylvania State University, 1987.

————. *Connections: Science by Writing*. Paradise, Calif.: Serin House Publishers, 1990.

Graves, Donald. H. *Writing: Teachers and Children at Work*. Portsmouth, N.H.: Heinemann Educational Books, 1982.

Haggerty, E., ed. dir. *Scholastic Scope English Writing and Language*. New York: Scholastic, 1990.

Hart, Leslie. *Human Brain and Human Learning*. New Rochelle, N.Y.: Brain Age Publishers, 1983.

Jones, Beau Fly, et al. *Strategic Teaching and Learning: Cognitive Instruction in Content Areas*. Alexandria, Va.: Association for Supervision and Curriculum Development, 1987.

Kneedler, Peter, "Statewide Assessment in History/Social Science Grade Eight: Why and What Happened," *Social Studies Review*, Winter 1986, Vol. 25:2, pp. 2–16.

Macrorie, Ken. *Telling Writing*. Upper Montclair, N.J.: Boynton/Cook Publishers, 1985.

Marzano, Robert, et al. *Dimensions of Thinking: A Framework for Curriculum and Instruction*. Alexandria, Va.: Association for Supervision and Curriculum Development, 1988.

Messick, Rosemary G., and Karen E. Reynolds, *Middle Level Curriculum in Action*. New York: Longman Publishing Group, 1992.

Moffett, James, *Active Voice: A Writing Program Across the Curriculum*. Upper Montclair, N.J.: Boynton/Cook Publishers, 1981.

Murray, Donald M. *A Writer Teaches Writing*. Boston: Houghton Mifflin, 1985.

Paul, Ricard, et al. *Critical Thinking Handbook, 6th–9th Grades: A Guide for Remodeling Lesson Plans in Language Arts, Social Studies and Science*, Sonoma, Calif.: Center for Critical Thinking and Moral Critique, 1989.

Rakow, Steven J., ed., "Special Supplement on Assessment," Science Scope, Washington, D.C.: NSTA, March, 1992.

Shay, Sandy. Personal communication, 1992.

Talbot, Jan, "The Assessment of Critical Thinking in History/Social Science Through Writing," *Social Studies Review,* Winter 1986, Vol. 25:2, pp. 33–41.

Tsruda, Gary. Asilomar math conference workshop, 1992.

Wells, Joel. Personal communication, 1992.